# THE GOOD THAT MEN CAN DO

# THE GOOD THAT MEN CAN DO

## D. Todd Christofferson

DESERET
BOOK

SALT LAKE CITY, UTAH

Book design © Deseret Book Company
Art direction: Richard Erickson
Design: Sheryl Dickert Smith

**Library of Congress Cataloging-in-Publication Data**

CIP on file

ISBN 978-1-62972-352-5

Printed in South Korea

Four Color Print Group, Paju-si, Gyeonggi-do

10   9   8   7   6   5   4   3   2   1

With deepest gratitude to my
shining example of the
good that men can do—Dad
Paul V. Christofferson, DVM

Fathers are fundamental in the divine plan of happiness. I want to raise a voice of encouragement for those who are striving to fill well that calling. I wish to focus on the good that men can do in the highest of masculine roles:

⇒ HUSBAND AND FATHER. ⇐

David Blankenhorn, the author of *Fatherless America*, has observed: "Today, American society is fundamentally divided and ambivalent about the fatherhood idea. Some people do not even remember it. Others are offended by it. Others, including more than a few family scholars, neglect it or disdain it. Many others are not especially opposed to it, nor are they especially committed to it. Many people wish we could act on it, but believe that our society simply no longer can or will."[1]

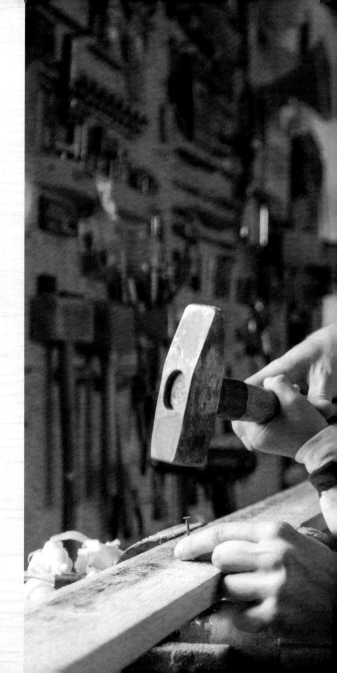

As a Church,

WE BELIEVE IN

# FATHERS.

## WE BELIEVE IN

{ "the ideal of the man who

puts his family first."[2] }

WE BELIEVE THAT

"**BY DIVINE DESIGN,**

fathers are to preside over their families

IN LOVE
AND
RIGHTEOUSNESS

and are responsible to provide
the necessities of life and protection
for their families."[3]

# WE BELIEVE THAT

in their complementary family duties,

"**fathers** and **mothers**

are obligated to help one another as

EQUAL

**partners.**"[4]

We believe that, far from being superfluous,

FATHERS

are

unique and
**IRREPLACEABLE.**

Some see the good of fatherhood in social terms, as something that obligates men to their offspring, impelling them to be good citizens and to think about the needs of others, supplementing "maternal investment in children with paternal investment in children. . . .

IN SHORT,

THE KEY FOR MEN IS TO
**be fathers.**

THE KEY FOR CHILDREN IS TO
**have fathers.**

THE KEY FOR SOCIETY IS TO
**create fathers."**[5]

While these considerations
are certainly true and
important, we know that
fatherhood is much more
than a social construct or
the product of evolution.
The role of father is of
divine origin, beginning
with a Father in Heaven
and, in this mortal sphere,
with Father Adam.

The perfect, divine expression of fatherhood is our Heavenly Father. His character and attributes include abundant goodness and perfect love. His work and glory are the development, happiness, and eternal life of His children.[6] Fathers in this fallen world can claim nothing comparable to the Majesty on High, but at their best, they are striving to emulate Him, and they indeed labor in His work. They are honored with a remarkable and sobering trust.

FOR MEN,

# fatherhood

exposes us to

our own weaknesses

AND OUR NEED TO
# improve.

# FATHERHOOD

## REQUIRES SACRIFICE,

but it is a source of

## INCOMPARABLE SATISFACTION,

even joy.

Again, the ultimate model is our Heavenly Father, who so loved us, His spirit children, that He gave us His Only Begotten Son for our salvation and exaltation.[7] Jesus said, "Greater love hath no man than this, that a man lay down his life for his friends."[8] Fathers manifest that love as they lay down their lives day by day, laboring in the service and support of their families.

Perhaps the most essential of a father's work is to turn the hearts of his children to their Heavenly Father. If by his example as well as his words a father can demonstrate what fidelity to God looks like in day-to-day living, that father will have given his children the key to peace in this life and eternal life in the world to come.[9]

# A FATHER

who reads scripture

---

## TO AND WITH HIS CHILDREN

---

acquaints them with

## THE VOICE OF THE LORD.[10]

We find in the scriptures a repeated emphasis on the parental obligation to teach one's children:

"And again, inasmuch as parents have children in Zion, or in any of her stakes which are organized, that teach them not to understand the doctrine of repentance, faith in Christ the Son of the living God, and of baptism and the gift of the Holy Ghost by the laying on of the hands, when eight years old, the sin be upon the heads of the parents. . . .

"And they shall also teach their children to pray, and to walk uprightly before the Lord."[11]

In 1833, the Lord reprimanded members of the First Presidency for inadequate attention to the duty of teaching their children. To one He said specifically, "You have not taught your children light and truth, according to the commandments; and that wicked one hath power, as yet, over you, and this is the cause of your affliction."[12]

Fathers are to teach God's law and works anew to each generation. As the Psalmist declared:

"For he established a testimony in Jacob, and appointed a law in Israel, which he commanded our fathers, that they should make them known to their children:

"That the generation to come might know them, even the children which should be born; who should [then] arise and declare them to their children:

"That they might set their hope in God, and not forget the works of God, but keep his commandments."[13]

Certainly teaching the gospel is a shared duty between fathers and mothers, but the Lord is clear that He expects fathers to lead out in making it a high priority.

(And let's remember that INFORMAL CONVERSATIONS, WORKING and PLAYING TOGETHER, and LISTENING are important elements of **teaching.**)

The Lord expects fathers to

# HELP SHAPE THEIR CHILDREN,

children want and need

# A MODEL.

I myself was blessed with an exemplary father. I recall that when I was a boy of about twelve, my father became a candidate for the city council in our rather small community. He did not mount an extensive election campaign—all I remember was that Dad had my brothers and me distribute copies of a flyer door-to-door, urging people to vote for Paul Christofferson. There were a number of adults that I handed a flyer to who remarked that Paul was a good and honest man and that they would have no problem voting for him. My young boy heart swelled with pride in my father. It gave me confidence and a desire to follow in his footsteps.

**HE WAS NOT PERFECT**

—no one is—

but he was upright

and good and an

aspirational example

for a son.

Discipline and correction are part of teaching. As Paul said, "For whom the Lord loveth he chasteneth."[14] But in discipline a father must exercise particular care, lest there be anything even approaching abuse, which is never justified. When a father provides correction, his motivation must be love and his guide the Holy Spirit:

"Reproving betimes with sharpness, when moved upon by the Holy Ghost; and then showing forth afterwards an increase of love toward him whom thou hast reproved, lest he esteem thee to be his enemy;

"That he may know that thy faithfulness is stronger than the cords of death."[15]

# DISCIPLINE

in the divine pattern is

not so much about

punishing as it is about

## HELPING A LOVED ONE

ALONG THE PATH OF

SELF-MASTERY.

THE LORD HAS SAID THAT

"all children have claim upon their parents for their maintenance until they are of age."[16] Breadwinning is a consecrated activity. Providing for one's family, although it generally requires time away from the family, is not inconsistent with fatherhood—it is the essence of being a good father.

# "**WORK** AND **FAMILY** are overlapping domains."[17]

This, of course, does not justify a man who neglects his family for his career or, at the other extreme, one who will not exert himself and is content to shift his responsibility to others. In the words of King Benjamin:

> "Ye will not suffer your children that they go hungry, or naked;
>
> neither will ye suffer that they transgress the laws of God,
>
> and fight and quarrel one with another. . . .
>
> "But ye will teach them to walk in the ways of truth and soberness;
>
> ye will teach them to love one another, and to serve one another."[18]

We recognize the agony of men who are unable to find ways and means adequately to sustain their families. There is no shame for those who, at a given moment, despite their best efforts, cannot fulfill all the duties and functions of fathers. "Disability, death, or other circumstances may necessitate individual adaptation. Extended families should lend support when needed."[19]

LOVING THE MOTHER OF HIS CHILDREN—

AND SHOWING THAT LOVE—

are two of the best things a father can do

# FOR HIS CHILDREN.

This reaffirms and strengthens

## ↣THE MARRIAGE↢

that is the foundation of their

family life and security.

Some men are single fathers, foster fathers, or stepfathers. Many of them strive mightily and do their very best in an often difficult role. We honor those who do all that can be done in love, patience, and self-sacrifice to meet individual and family needs. It should be noted that God Himself entrusted His Only Begotten Son to a foster father. Surely some of the credit goes to Joseph for the fact that as Jesus grew, He "increased in wisdom and stature, and in favour with God and man."[20]

Regrettably, due to death, abandonment, or divorce, some children don't have fathers living with them. Some may have fathers who are physically present but emotionally absent or in other ways inattentive or nonsupportive. We call on all fathers to do better and to be better. We call on media and entertainment outlets to portray devoted and capable fathers who truly love their wives and intelligently guide their children, instead of the bumblers and buffoons or "the guys who cause problems," as fathers are all too frequently depicted.

To children whose family situation is troubled, we say, you yourself are no less for that. Challenges are at times an indication of the Lord's trust in you. He can help you, directly and through others, to deal with what you face. You can become the generation, perhaps the first in your family, where the divine patterns that God has ordained for families truly take shape and bless all the generations after you.

To young men, recognizing the role you will have as provider and protector, we say, prepare now by being diligent in school and planning for postsecondary training. Education, whether in a university, technical school, apprenticeship, or similar program, is key to developing the skills and capabilities you will need. Take advantage of opportunities to associate with people of all ages, including children, and learn how to establish healthy and rewarding relationships. That typically means talking face-to-face with people and sometimes doing things together, not just perfecting your texting skills. Live your life so that as a man you will bring purity to your marriage and to your children.

To all the rising generation, we say, wherever you rank your own father on the scale of good-better-best (and I predict that ranking will go higher as you grow older and wiser), make up your mind to honor him and your mother by your own life. Remember the yearning hope of a father as expressed by John: "I have no greater joy than to hear that my children walk in truth."[21] Your righteousness is the greatest honor any father can receive.

To my brethren, the fathers in this Church, I say, I know you wish you were a more perfect father. I know I wish I were. Even so, despite our limitations, let us press on. Let us lay aside the exaggerated notions of individualism and autonomy in today's culture and think first of the happiness and well-being of others.

Surely, despite our

inadequacies,

our Heavenly Father will magnify us

and cause our

simple efforts to bear fruit.

I am encouraged by a story that appeared in the *New Era* some years ago. The author recounted the following:

"When I was young, our little family lived in a one-bedroom apartment on the second floor. I slept on the couch in the living room. . . . My dad, a steelworker, left home very early for work each day. Every morning he would . . . tuck the covers around me and stop for a minute. I would be half-dreaming when I could sense my dad standing beside the couch, looking at me. As I slowly awoke, I became embarrassed to have him there. I tried to pretend I was still asleep. . . . I became aware that as he stood beside my bed he was praying with all his attention, energy, and focus—for me.

"Each morning my dad prayed for me. He prayed that I would have a good day, that I would be safe, that I would learn and prepare for the future. And since he could not be with me until evening, he prayed for the teachers and my friends that I would be with that day. . . .

"At first, I didn't really understand what my dad was doing those mornings when he prayed for me. . . . It wasn't until years later, after I was married, had children of my own, and would go into their rooms while they were asleep and pray for them that I understood completely how my father felt about me."[22]

## ALMA TESTIFIED TO HIS SON:

"Behold, I say unto you, that it is [Christ] that surely shall come . . . ; yea he cometh to declare glad tidings of salvation unto his people.

"And now, my son, this was the ministry unto which ye were called, to declare these glad tidings unto this people, to prepare their minds; or rather . . . that they may prepare the minds of their children to hear the word at the time of his coming."[23]

That is the ministry of fathers today. God bless and make them equal to it.

# SOURCES

1. David Blankenhorn, *Fatherless America: Confronting Our Most Urgent Social Problem* (New York: Basic Books, 1995), 62.

2. Blankenhorn, *Fatherless America*, 5.

3. "The Family: A Proclamation to the World," *Ensign*, November 2010, 129.

4. "The Family: A Proclamation to the World," 129.

5. Blankenhorn, *Fatherless America*, 25, 26.

6. See Moses 1:39.

7. See John 3:16.

8. John 15:13.

9. See Doctrine and Covenants 59:23; Moses 6:59.

10. See Doctrine and Covenants 18:34–36.

11. Doctrine and Covenants 68:25, 28.

12. Doctrine and Covenants 93:42.

13. Psalm 78:5–7.

14. Hebrews 12:6.

15. Doctrine and Covenants 121:43–44.

16. Doctrine and Covenants 83:4.

17. Blankenhorn, *Fatherless America*, 113.

18. Mosiah 4:14–15.

19. "The Family: A Proclamation to the World," 129.

20. Luke 2:52.

21. 3 John 1:4.

22. Julian Dyke, "Thanks, Dad," *New Era*, April 1993, 38.

23. Alma 39:15–16.

# PHOTO CREDITS

# ABOUT THE AUTHOR

Elder D. Todd Christofferson was called to the Quorum of the Twelve Apostles of The Church of Jesus Christ of Latter-day Saints on April 5, 2008. At the time of his call, he was serving in the Presidency of the Seventy.

Born in Pleasant Grove, Utah, Elder Christofferson graduated from high school in New Jersey, and he served a mission in Argentina. He then went on to earn his bachelor's degree from Brigham Young University and his law degree from Duke University.

Prior to his service as a full-time General Authority of the Church, Elder Christofferson was associate general counsel of NationsBank Corporation (now Bank of America) in Charlotte, North Carolina. Previously, he was senior vice president and general counsel for Commerce Union Bank of Tennessee in Nashville, where he was also active in community affairs and interfaith organizations. From 1975 to 1980, Elder Christofferson practiced law in Washington, D.C., after serving as a law clerk to U.S. District Judge John J. Sirica from 1972 to 1974.

Elder Christofferson and his wife, Katherine Jacob Christofferson, are the parents of five children.